Toby the Tiger Tamer

By
Amy Johnson Reamer

Illustrations by Kayla Brazier

ISBN: 978-1484099889

Design: Dedicated Book Services, Inc. (www.netdbs.com)

This book is dedicated to the first clients who worked with me to tame their own tigers—especially KL, and to my wonderful husband and 3 children—who have met my Tiger one too many times :)

I'm excited about working with many more tiger tamers.

A big thank you to my cousin Kayla who worked very hard on the fabulous colorful illustrations for this book.

I look forward to seeing her future artwork.

Hi, my name is Toby—nice to meet you. I'm a pretty regular kid. I live with my little sister and my mom. I like to play soccer and draw pictures. My dad doesn't live with us anymore. Since my dad left I've been in a lot of trouble. I learned some things that helped me a lot though. This is the story about how I became a Tiger tamer.

I was in trouble—again. This time it was for throwing something at my sister. Last time it was for yelling at my teacher. The time before that it was for running away from home after getting in trouble for something else. I have been told lots of good things to do instead of the things that get me in trouble. The problem is—I never seem to remember to do those things until it is too late.

I'm sorry afterwards and promise never to do it again—and I mean it! The trouble just keeps coming back. I was so confused and I felt so powerless against the trouble. I wondered if I would ever get all of these feelings that lead to trouble under control.

Over the holidays my cousin Leah came to visit. Leah is in college and she is studying the brain and how it works. I was looking at her books on the brain and thought it was so cool but all of the big long words were boring and hard to remember. So Leah told me about the Tiger, the Hippo and the Owl.

"You see Toby, the Tiger is the part of the brain that helps keep us safe. When your Tiger sees, hears, smells, feels or tastes something new or different it has to make sure there's no danger. Or it could sense something it recognizes from before, like the car accident you and your mom were in last year, was a scary thing. When you hear the car horns your Tiger thinks the scary thing is happening again."

If the Tiger feels like there's any danger it will want you to fight, run or freeze to help protect you. The Tiger doesn't think—it just acts. The Owl does our thinking. It helps us to solve problems, make decisions and helps us use words. The other important part is the Hippo. The Hippo helps us to learn by swallowing the information we take in from all around us and it works with the Owl to help the Tiger calm down.

6

Cortex

Twl

Amygdala

Tiger

HippoCampus

The Hippo is really important in school but it's with us all the time to help with learning and working with the Owl and Tiger. Usually the 3 of them work well together, talking to each other to keep us safe, learning new things and making good decisions. Sometimes though, they just don't work together very well.

Especially if the Tiger gets woken up a lot when we are really little (maybe adults did not do a good job keeping us safe or a lot of scary things happened to us or around us), he becomes a really light sleeper. Instead of just waking up a little—he wakes up with a roar! Instead of just waking up when there's real danger, he wakes up at other times too. This makes the Owl fly away and the Hippo hides under the water!

If the Owl flies away we can't think, we can't use words very well and we can't make many decisions at all! If the Hippo is hiding we can't learn new things or remember what people say to us when our Tiger is roaring. The Tiger now might think it has to be in charge all of the time. It starts sensing danger a lot of the time, even when there really isn't any and it stops listening to the Owl and the Hippo.

"If our Tiger gets woken up a lot in school, we may have trouble learning or listening and following directions. At home we may get into trouble for fighting with our brothers and sisters or not listening to our parents." "So how do we get rid of the Tiger if it's always causing trouble" I asked. Leah replied "Not so fast—We all need a Tiger because we need to be able to fight back or run when we really need to stay safe.

So we don't want to get rid of our Tiger—we just need to tame it!"
I was so excited—this was starting to make sense! "I want to tame
my Tiger!" I said with excitement. Leah asked "So what usually
makes your Tiger wake up?" I thought for a minute and said, "My
Tiger does not like loud noises so when my sister squeals and
screams at me he sometimes wakes up."

"Best Buddy"

toby

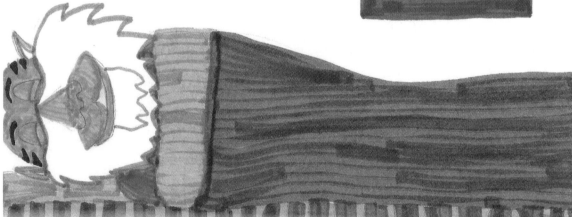

"How do you know he's waking up? "My head is hurting and my hands feel tight." "What does he do when he wakes up?" "He makes me want to yell at her and throw things to make her stop." So then Leah asked "What makes your Tiger go back to sleep?" This was a tough question. I wasn't really sure. So Leah asked "Where do you feel safe? Or who do you feel safe with?" I said "I feel safe in my bedroom."

Leah told me to try the next time I feel my Tiger waking up, to picture myself in my bedroom, and imagine everything I see in my room, what I hear and what I smell when I'm in my bedroom. Leah then said "You also said your hands feel tight when your Tiger wakes up, let's practice making tight fists, with both your hands, open them, shake them out and tighten them again.

Practice with Toby and Leah!

Let's practice this now, while your Tiger is sleeping so it will be easier to remember to try when he's waking up. I'll try it with you." Leah also told me, "You can talk to your Tiger, let him know you are ok, to curl up and go back to sleep." Leah explained "To become a Tiger tamer it takes time and practice. Not everyone's Tiger wakes up to the same things and not everyone's Tiger goes back to sleep from the same things."

"Sometimes when our Tigers wake up, they wake up the Tigers of those around us too. If parents, teachers and other adults can keep their Tigers calm they could help your Tiger learn how to calm down too. Just like adults teach kids lots of things, their Tigers can teach our Tiger cubs to roar—or to purr."

So I started paying attention to when my body would tell me my Tiger was waking up and I practiced some of the things Leah taught me. In class when I would get frustrated and I could feel my heart beating fast, and my head was hurting and my hands felt so tight—I would start to open and close my hands and I would tell that Tiger "It's only a test, I'm ok, you can go back to sleep." And guess what—it worked!

My head stopped hurting and I could remember the spelling words I studied. The Owl came back and the Hippo came up out of the water!

One day, at home, my sister was squealing and chasing me and I picked up a toy truck and was going to throw it at her. My mom gave me a hug and said, "Toby, I know the loud noises wake up your Tiger, tell him you're ok, and I'll help you and your sister." I realized hugs from my mom help my Tiger feel safe too.

So even though I still get in trouble sometimes, it doesn't happen very often at all anymore. Most of the time when my Tiger gets stirred I'm able to do something to help it go back to sleep that

doesn't get me in trouble. I realized that throwing things, yelling or running away was how I used to make my Tiger feel safe.

Changing what I did to calm my Tiger was hard sometimes, but after a lot of practice when I was calm, with the help of my parents and teachers—I became a Tiger tamer really quickly!

So what did you think of my story?

What wakes up your Tiger?

What does your Tiger want you to do to feel safe?

What do you or others do to help your Tiger go back to sleep?

What things make your Tiger roar louder, or want to run and hide?

What does your dad's Tiger do when it wakes up?

Can you draw a picture of your Tiger awake? How about sleeping? I wonder what your Owl says to the Tiger to get it to calm down.

Get to know your Tiger—it's a part of you!

You may need to get some help from your parents, teachers, counselors or other people who you feel safe with practicing and trying different things. Soon you will find what works for your Tiger and doesn't hurt yourself, other people or things. Pretty soon your Tiger, Hippo and Owl will be working together like a team again and you can call yourself a "Tiger Tamer!"

To parents, teachers and other caregivers of children—

By understanding our own bodies and nervous systems and those of our children we can help their systems develop and grow and be able to regulate their own emotions over time. By recognizing and addressing the child's fear lying underneath the behaviors you will help to calm their Tiger and they will be better able to listen to you and follow your directions. Many behaviors you see children doing are maladaptive ways to help themselves feel safer and either get away from or stop whatever is making them feel unsafe. Without realizing it our own words or actions can be making their fear worse instead of making them feel safe. Their actions and words can wake up our own Tigers and we start reacting. Once everyone's Tigers are sleeping again then lessons can be learned and messages heard. Taming your own Tiger in many of the same ways Toby learned in this story will lead to better interactions with your child or student and lower everyone's reactivity.

Words belong to the Owl, so until you can get the Tiger back to sleep and the Owl returns and the Hippo surfaces—complex words, messages or directions will not be heard or understood. Use short reassuring messages when a child is becoming dysregulated (Tiger is fully awake) to help them feel safe again. Try sitting down and just being quiet and breathing. Slow deep breaths are a first step. Tame your own Tiger before you try to help a child tame theirs!

About the Author—

Amy is passionate about helping others heal their hearts from past hurts—through the use of research and evidence based practices infused with the latest neuroscience research. She has personal and professional experience with adoption, parent training and providing therapy services. She has a Bachelor's of Science degree in Human Services Management and a Master's of Science Degree in Marriage and Family Therapy/Counseling (MFT) and a post-baccalaureate certificate in Psychology—Play Therapy Specialization. She is a self-proclaimed "brain geek" and continuously finds fun ways to incorporate the latest neuroscience research into evidence-based practices specializing in the effects of early trauma or neglect on the brain and the best ways to help children and teenagers heal from this. She is currently in her residency in MFT working towards licensure as a marriage and family therapist in Virginia as well as pursuing the credential of registered play therapist. She is a certified TLC Level 1 Trauma Specialist and has completed Level 1 Training in Theraplay. In addition to the use of play, art and other expressive modalities Amy uses Solution Focused, Narrative, Gestalt and Emotionally Focused Therapy Models with individuals and families. She is the owner and clinical director of Heart and Mind Therapy Services, LLC in the Richmond, VA area—a group practice of professionals with different specialties and strengths—all dedicated to being a part of the healing journey of others.